GREEK ISLAND MYTHS

TINOS
THE MIRACLE-WORKING ICON

JILL DUDLEY

PUT IT IN YOUR POCKET SERIES
ORPINGTON PUBLISHERS

Published by
Orpington Publishers

Cover design and origination by
Creeds, Bridport, Dorset
01308 423411

Printed and bound in the UK by
Creeds

© Jill Dudley 2017

ISBN: 978-0-9935378-9-9

TINOS

THE MIRACLE-WORKING ICON

Tinos is one of the Cycladic islands famous for its Church of Panagia Evangelistria which stands on a hilltop some eight hundred metres up from the port with a wide cobbled road going up to it.

It is an imposing building with two arcaded levels to which wide balustraded stairways ascend either side. Below its ornate cornice are arched windows. Before Christianity there was once a temple of Dionysos on the site – Dionysos, god of wine and drama – and there was an amphitheatre to one side below it.

The church is the proud possessor of a miracle-working icon of the Virgin Mary. Twice a year, on the feast-day of the Annunciation of the Virgin Mary (March 25th) and the Assumption of the Virgin Mary (August 15th), invalids crowd into the church where they spend the night in the hope of a miraculous cure. During the summer months many pilgrims who have had their prayers answered show their humility and gratitude by crawling on hands and knees from the port up the eight hundred metres of cobbled road to the icon in the church; strips of carpet are laid up the hill for the greater comfort of these pious people.

The icon itself is only eighteen inches high but, like a diminutive monarch, is made to look majestic by its large ornate arched frame overlaid with strings of pearls and precious stones, allowing only the face of the Virgin Mary to be visible. It is placed on a large marble pillared stand near to the church entrance. It is the goal for those arriving on hands and knees who, once inside, get to their feet, cross themselves in the Orthodox manner, and reverently kiss the glass over the icon.

The icon has a long history. In the tenth century Saracen pirates destroyed an earlier church which stood on the site of the present one, and the icon was lost. It was not redisovered till 1823 when a nun had repeated visions of the Virgin Mary commanding her to dig for the lost icon.

The nun, Agia Pelagia, first thought she might be hallucinating, or that it was the devil speaking, and so said nothing. It was not until the third vision when the Virgin Mary began to be angry, that she started fearing the Virgin more than being thought a fool and reported the matter. When the Bishop was informed, he immediately ordered that digging should commence and the whole island joined in with enthusiasm.

After several months passed and no icon was found, they began to lose interest and the work petered out. Soon there was an epidemic and hundreds died, so the bishop ordered that digging should recommence. As soon as they went to work again the epidemic ended.

The search had started in the autumn of 1822. At the end of January 1823, one of the islanders felt his spade strike something. He discovered that he had split a piece of wood in half and the first piece he took from the ground depicted the Angel Gabriel presenting a lily to a missing figure. He then took out the second piece and found it portrayed the Virgin Mary in a room kneeling before a *prie-dieu* on which was an open book with the words of the Annunciation. A dove, representing the Holy Spirit, was included in the scene. Amazingly, although it had been in the ground for over eight hundred years, it was in an excellent state of preservation.

Because the nun had had her vision at the start of the War of Independence and the icon had been recovered a few months later, the icon became identified with Greek freedom and liberation from Turkish rule. Money had poured in from all quarters of Greece and the Orthodox world to help build a new church for the icon. No expense was spared and, whenever money began to run short, the labourers were happy to work on without salaries until more donations arrived.

The interior of the church is magnificent. Heavy silver chandeliers hang down amidst dozens of icon lamps with a silver or gold attachment depicting a leg, a ship, a house, a child, a cow, a mule, each representing the gratitude of some pilgrim whose prayers have been answered. Hundreds of candles of supplication cast their shadowy light and reflect off marble, silver, gold and gleaming brass.

On the eve of a festival of the Virgin Mary invalids spend the night in the gallery of the church, or in dormitories around the cloisters. A Vigil is held and the invalids receive holy unction. On the feast-day itself bishops and priests attend the liturgy, after which those invalids who are able to, form a column outside the church, and the icon is carried out on its gold and silver ciborium (canopied shrine) and passed over the heads of the sick and disabled. It is followed by a brass band and a procession of priests, bishops, island dignitaries, units from the armed forces, and school children. They descend to the port where the V.I.P.s gather on a dais and all turn towards the church while prayers are said amidst chanting, and the pealing of the church bells.

It is interesting that the icon is believed to have been painted by St. Luke – St. Luke the physician. If St. Luke was a healer, it should not be surprising that his icon imparts his curative powers. And St. Luke would, surely, have known the Virgin Mary. If so, he would have painted a true likeness of her.

Agia Pelagia was a nun from the Convent of Kechrovouni, some ten kilometres from the port high up in the hills. To get there you pass several of the famous Tinian dovecotes, large whitewashed buildings whose upper halves have a smocking-like decoration. It is possible to visit the nun's cell and chapel there. Her small cell contains a narrow bed, a candlestick, and a large painting on a wall depicting her on her knees to the vision of the Virgin Mary.

Before Christianity, rather strangely, it was Poseidon, god of the sea, who was accredited with healing powers on Tinos. A few kilometres to the west of the port are the remains of a temple dedicated to him and his wife Amphitrite, a Nereid, or sea-goddess. In pagan times Poseidon had been known as the 'doctor of Tinos' and his wife had been beseeched regarding fertility problems.

All changed with the coming of Christianity, and the recovery of the lost icon. Now the Virgin Mary is appealed to for both fertility and for the cure of ailments. Candles of differing lengths can be bought from the many booths lining the cobbled road ascending to the church. Some are as long as two metres, and are lit in the grotto marking the site where the miraculous icon was unearthed.

Numerous young couples come to this great church bringing their infants to be baptized. Baptisms take place in the crypt where there are several gleaming copper baptismal fonts fitted with taps and plumbed to the ground. Down there is a marble basin with a marble plaque above it depicting the Virgin and Child; it marks the spot where there was once a spring that had run dry. But on the day when the foundation stone of this new church was being laid, the Archbishop sent a child off with a bucket to fetch water for the formal blessing, and the child had run back to say that the spring was miraculously flowing again.

As for miraculous healings, well, there have been many.

There was the mother whose child suffered from severe eczema and, after sleeping the night in the church and being annointed with holy oil, the eczema gradually faded. There have been deaf people who have heard, blind people who have seen, a woman dying of a brain tumour who survived. And so the list goes on.

Apart from its great church and its miracle-working icon, the island is as any other island, a hive of activity by summer with ferry-boats disgorging their many passengers and taking on others, and many tavernas lining the sea-front with the colourful fishing boats and yachts moored up along the quayside. Every Greek island has something unique about it, and Tinos? Well, it has its icon.

MORE FROM THE
PUT IT IN YOUR POCKET SERIES

TROJAN WAR
THE JUDGEMENT OF PARIS
HELEN
KING AGAMEMNON
ACHILLES
THE WOODEN HORSE
ODYSSEUS

SACRED SITES
ATHENS – THE ACROPOLIS
CORINTH – ST. PAUL AND THE GODDESS OF LOVE
DELPHI – THE ORACLE OF APOLLO
ELEUSIS – DEMETER AND KORE
EPIDAURUS – CENTRE OF HEALING
OLYMPIA – THE OLYMPIC GAMES

ALSO BY JILL DUDLEY

YE GODS! (TRAVELS IN GREECE)
YE GODS! II (MORE TRAVELS IN GREECE)
LAP OF THE GODS (TRAVELS IN CRETE
AND THE AEGEAN ISLANDS)